Countries Around the World

Israel

Claire Throp

Heinemann Library
Chicago, Illinois

© 2012 Heinemann Library
an imprint of Capstone Global Library, LLC
Chicago, Illinois

Edited by Catherine Veitch and Charlotte Guillain
Designed by Steve Mead
Original illustrations © Capstone Global Library Ltd 2012
Illustrated by Oxford Designers & Illustrators
Picture research by Hannah Taylor
Originated by Capstone Global Library Ltd
Printed in China by CTPS

15 14 13 12 11
10 9 8 7 6 5 4 3 2 1

Library of Congress Cataloging-in-Publication Data
Throp, Claire.
   Israel / Claire Throp.
      p. cm.—(Countries around the world)
   Includes bibliographical references and index.
   ISBN 978-1-4329-6101-5 (hb)—ISBN 978-1-4329-6127-5 (pb) 1.
Israel. 2. Israel—Juvenile literature. I. Title.
   DS126.5.T497 2011
   956.94—dc22   2011015803

Acknowledgments
We would like to thank the following for permission to reproduce photographs: Alamy Images pp. 25 (© Alex Segre), 28 (© Israel Images), 34 (© M.Sobreira); Corbis pp. 7 (The Gallery Collection), 11 (Thomas Hartwell), 12 (Reuters/Paul Hanna), 13 (EPA/MICHAEL REYNOLDS), 16 (EPA/JIM HOLLANDER), 27 (EPA/JIM HOLLANDER), 31 (Hanan Isachar/AWL Images Ltd), 39 (Bettmann); Dreamstime p. 18 (© Smellme); Getty Images pp. 8 (AFP), 30 (AFP); Istockphoto pp. 20 (© kavram), 21 (© nitsan avivi), 22 (© Elena Zapassky); Shutterstock pp. 5 (© Yevgenia Gorbulsky), 14 (© Roman Sigaev), 19 (© hagit berkovich), 24 (© NEO), 29 (© Dmitry Pistrov), 33 (© bonchan), 35 (© Ryan Rodrick Beiler), 37 (© AlexGul).

Cover photograph of a Jewish person praying at the Wailing Wall, Jerusalem, Israel, reproduced with permission of Photolibrary (Imagebroker.net/ Fabian von Poser).

Every effort has been made to contact copyright holders of material reproduced in this book. Any omissions will be rectified in subsequent printings if notice is given to the publisher.

The author and publishers would like to thank Dr. Colin Shindler and Marta Segal Block for their invaluable assistance in the preparation of this book.

Disclaimer

Contents

Some words in the book are in bold, **like this**. You can find out what they mean by looking in the glossary.

Introducing Israel

When you think of Israel, what comes to mind? Famous places, such as the Western Wall, Bethlehem, and the Dead Sea? The country's food or range of different environments and wildlife? Or the conflict with the Palestinians? Israel is famous for these things and more.

Israel is in the Middle East, located at the meeting point of three continents— Europe, Africa, and Asia. It is about the same size as New Jersey, with a population of around 7.4 million. Israel is among the wealthier countries in the Middle East. This is due to its large number of high-tech industries and its **trade** links with the United States and Europe. Israel is bordered by Lebanon, Syria, Egypt, Jordan, and the Mediterranean Sea.

Religion

Israel is important for three separate religions, because there are holy sites for Jewish, Muslim, and Christian people in the capital city, Jerusalem. This is part of the reason for the ongoing troubles in the region.

A modern state

Israel is a young country, but the Jewish people have been linked to the area for thousands of years. Israel now is a place that Jews call home. Palestinians, however, believe the region is their home, too. Palestinians are the non-Jewish people who lived on this land before Israel was formed. This situation has led to conflict.

How to say...

The two main languages in Israel are Hebrew and Arabic.
Both languages are written in alphabets that are different from English.

	Hebrew	**Arabic**
hello	*shalom* (sha-lom)	*ahlan* (ahh-lan)
see you later	*lehitra'ot* (le-hit-ra-ot)	*ila-liqaa* (illa-liqaa)

The Dome of the Rock is the oldest Islamic monument that stands today. It is located on a site that is of great religious importance to both Jewish and Muslim people.

History: The Fight for a Jewish State

Jewish people lived in the area that is now Israel from before 1250 BCE until the Bar-Kokhba revolt of 135 CE, when they were forced out of their country by the Romans. Other invasions followed—by the Byzantines, the Muslim Arabs, the European Christians, and the Ottoman Turks. Most Jews were scattered around the world.

The British mandate

In 1897 Theodor Herzl formed the **Zionist** movement, which said that Jews should have their own country in ancient Israel. After the Balfour Declaration made by the British government in 1917, thousands of Jews began to move to the area that was once ancient Israel. This declaration promised a national home for the Jewish people, as long as it did not affect the rights of the local, non-Jewish population.

The British and French were given **mandates** to rule the area by the **League of Nations**. From 1921 the British divided their area into Palestine, Transjordan, and Iraq. The Zionist Organization was chosen to represent Jewish people in Palestine. The Palestinian Arabs became worried about losing control of their lands as more and more Jews arrived.

The Holocaust

After Adolf Hitler became German leader in 1933, Jews in Germany, and then Jews in Nazi-controlled Europe, lost their rights, their businesses, and their homes. Nazi Germany tried to kill all European Jews during World War II (1939–45). They were sent to **concentration camps** and killed in **gas chambers**. Six million Jews died in the Holocaust—a third of all Jews in the world. After the State of Israel was created, many surviving European Jews went to live in Israel.

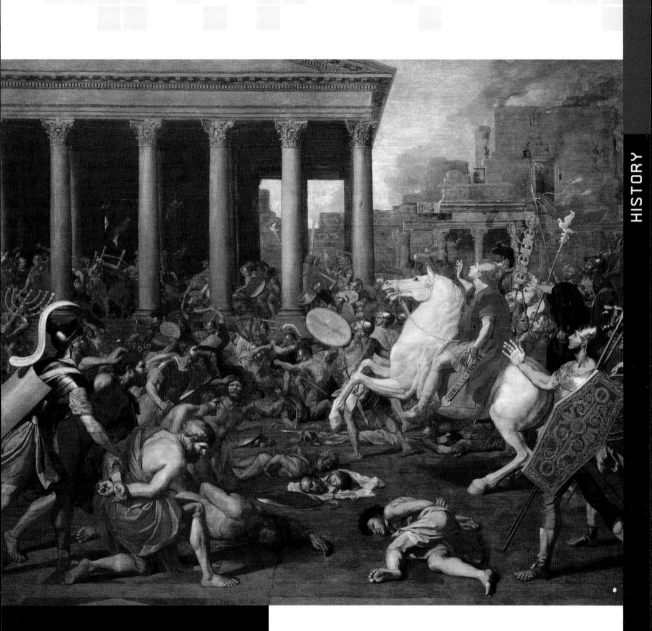

This painting shows an event that happened in 70 CE. Roman troops are destroying the Second Temple in Jerusalem.

Independence

In 1947 the British handed control of Palestine to the newly formed **United Nations (UN)**. The UN suggested dividing Palestine into two parts, between Palestinian Arabs and the Jewish people. The UN would control Jerusalem, because of its importance to both Jews and Arabs. The Jews agreed with the UN's plans, but the Arabs did not. However, when the British left in May 1948, the Zionist Jews announced the creation of the State of Israel.

David Ben-Gurion announced the creation of the State of Israel on May 14, 1948. In 1950 the Law of Return was created. It stated that any Jew can move to Israel and be given citizenship right away.

The Palestinian Arabs and the Arab countries of Egypt, Syria, Jordan, Lebanon, and Iraq fought against Israel in the following months. Israel won what the Jewish people there call their War of Independence.

At the beginning of the first Arab-Israeli War, about 900,000 Palestinians were living in what later became Israel. By early 1949, only 150,000 remained. These Palestinian Arabs then had to live under Israeli rule. Those who fled during the war were unable to return, and many were forced to live in **refugee** camps in the West Bank, Gaza, Lebanon, and Syria. The refugees often lived in awful conditions. The only Arab state willing to include the refugees within its society was Jordan. In other Arab countries, the refugees were **stateless**.

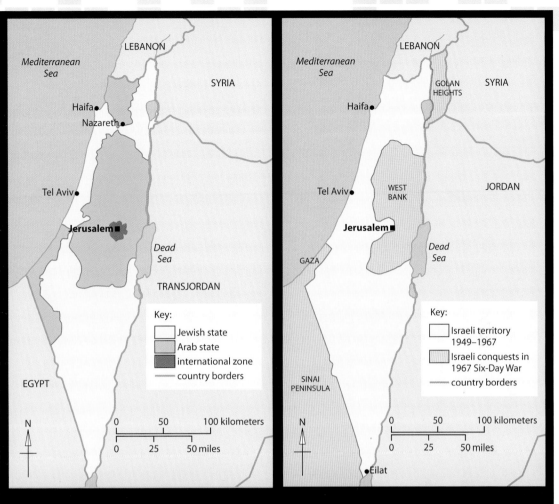

The map on the left shows how the UN suggested the land should be divided between the Jews and the Arabs in 1947. On the right, the map shows the actual territory held by the Israelis after their War of Independence, as well as the territory conquered by Israel in the Six-Day War of 1967.

Six-Day War, 1967

In June 1967, an attack by Egypt on Israel seemed likely. Expecting an attack, Israel decided to strike first by destroying Egypt's air force. Soon Syria and Jordan joined the fighting. In six days, Israel won a large amount of land, including the Sinai Peninsula, Golan Heights, the West Bank, and East Jerusalem. Israel expanded to four times its original size.

In 1967 the UN suggested that Israel give back the land it had taken, in return for peace with the Arab states. This did not happen, but it formed the basis of future peace discussions.

Israeli settlements

From 1968, **right-wing** and religious Israelis began to create **settlements** in areas such as the West Bank. This angered Palestinians, who had formed a group called the Palestinian Liberation Organization (PLO) to regain Palestine and end the State of Israel. They were prepared to use violence to do this. One PLO leader was Yasser Arafat.

War and terrorism

In the 1973 Yom Kippur War, Egypt attacked Israel. Israel pushed Egypt back, and a **cease-fire** followed. A few years later, President Sadat of Egypt visited Israel, offering a peace plan. Sinai was later returned to Egypt. However, in 1982 Israel invaded Lebanon, fearing a Palestinian attack on northern Israel. By 1987 Palestinians were desperate for their own state. They began a mass uprising against the Israeli occupation, known as the First **Intifada**. The uprising lasted for six years and cost many lives.

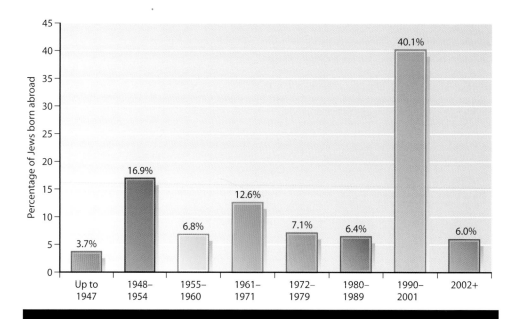

This chart shows the percentage of the Jewish population that has moved to Israel, by time period. **Immigration** from Russia boosted the population in the 1990s.

Oslo Accords

In the 1990s, peace talks were held in the United States and Oslo, Norway. Israeli **Prime Minister** Yitzhak Rabin and Palestinian leader Yasser Arafat signed an agreement that would have seen the withdrawal of Israeli forces from parts of the Gaza Strip and West Bank, with control passed over to the Palestinians. Arafat later became leader of the Palestinian Authority, the body set up to rule the Palestinian territories. However, Israel's right-wing Likud **political party** and some Palestinians were not happy. A Palestinian group, Hamas, used **suicide bombers** to ruin the peace process. A Jewish **extremist** murdered Rabin in 1995, further threatening peace talks.

YASSER ARAFAT (1929-2004)

Yasser Arafat was born (probably in Cairo, Egypt) in 1929 and moved to Jerusalem when he was five years old. He became leader of the PLO in the late 1960s and publicized the Palestinians' problems around the world. Along with Shimon Peres and Yitzhak Rabin, Arafat won the Nobel Peace Prize in 1994 for his efforts in the Oslo Accords. People wept in the streets in the Palestinian territories when he died in November 2004.

Security

In 2002 Israel built a security barrier around parts of the West Bank, blocking access to Jerusalem and parts of Israel. Israel said this was to secure their country from Palestinian attacks. Palestinians thought it was a way to gain more of their land. The United States proposed a "Road Map" for peace in 2003. Israelis were to stop building settlements in land that they occupied militarily, and Palestinians had to stop their violence. Neither of these demands was met, however.

Big changes

In August 2005, Ariel Sharon, prime minister and leader of the Likud, ordered the evacuation of 21 Israeli settlements in the Gaza Strip and the northern West Bank. The Gaza Strip was now entirely under Palestinian control. In November, he resigned as head of Likud and formed a new political party called Kadima. Kadima won the 2006 election. The 2006 election in the Palestinian Authority was won by Hamas. Hamas supporters had introduced suicide bombing, did not recognize Israel, and wished to replace Israel with a Palestinian state.

In 2005 not every Israeli living in the Gaza settlements wanted to leave. Some had to be forced from their homes by soldiers.

Peace talks

Yet more peace talks began in 2007, and they went well until December 2008. Then, Israel attacked Gaza, and talks were suspended. Israel said the attacks were in response to Palestinian rocket fire. However, other countries criticized Israel, as far more Palestinians than Israelis were killed. In September 2010, peace talks were finally restarted. Israeli Prime Minister Benjamin Netanyahu and Palestinian leader Mahmoud Abbas met in Washington, D.C.

Netanyahu, Abbas, and U.S. President Barack Obama were photographed as peace talks began again in September 2010.

Regions and Resources: A Diverse Country

There are four main geographical areas in Israel: the coastal plain, rolling hills and mountains, a **rift valley**, and desert.

Rivers and seas

The Jordan River flows through the rift valley along the east of the country and into the Dead Sea. It is a major water source for Israel, Jordan, Syria, and Lebanon. There are Arab and Jewish **settlements** along the river, including the Hula Valley and the oldest **kibbutz** in Israel, Degania. The Dead Sea is a lake rather than a sea, and it is famous for its high levels of salt. Lake Tiberias in the north is also known as the Sea of Galilee. It is the largest freshwater lake in Israel.

The Jordan River flows through Lake Tiberias.

Mountains and desert

Israel's highest mountain is Mount Meron, in Galilee. It is about 3,963 feet (1,208 meters) high. The Negev Desert in the south takes up 62 percent of Israel's land. A mountain range runs along the north of the Negev. Mount Ramon is the highest peak in the range, at 3,395 feet (1,035 meters).

Natural disasters

Israel is in an active earthquake zone, although it has been several hundred years since the last major earthquake. Flash floods can also occur.

Climate

Along the Mediterranean coast, Israel is generally hot, humid, and sunny, with a mild and wet winter from November to April. The north and east are less humid in the summer and have quite cold winters. The desert is nearly always hot and dry.

Key:
Land height above sea level:
- over 4900 feet
- over 3250 feet
- over 1650 feet
- over 650 feet
- below 650 feet
- below sea level
- —— country borders

LEBANON
SYRIA
GOLAN HEIGHTS
Mount Meron ▲
Haifa •
Lake Tiberias
Jordan River
JORDAN VALLEY
COASTAL PLAIN
WEST BANK
Tel Aviv •
Mediterranean Sea
CENTRAL MOUNTAINS
■ Jerusalem
Dead Sea
GAZA STRIP
JORDAN
ISRAEL
Negev Desert
▲ Mount Ramon
EGYPT

0   50   100 kilometers
0   25   50 miles

N

• Eilat

This map shows the physical features of Israel.

The economy

Israel was once a poor country, but it now has a standard of living similar to that of Western Europe. Israel was not badly affected by the global economic crisis that began in 2008. This was partly because the government had kept a tight control on the banking system in the years leading up to the crisis.

Daily life

Kibbutzim are farms that are jointly owned by the people who live there. Each farm is called a kibbutz. Everything is shared on a kibbutz, including work, decision-making, looking after children, food, and buildings. Today, products such as electrical goods are produced there, as well as agriculture. Moshavim are similar to kibbutzim, but the people who live there have more independence. Families live and work separately, but they get together to sell their produce.

These workers are sorting Merlot grapes on a kibbutz in Israel. The grapes will be made into wine.

Resources and trade

There are few natural **resources** in Israel. Its people have worked hard to develop the land for agriculture, despite a lack of water and much of the land being desert. The **immigration** of skilled workers has helped to improve Israel's industries. Israel has strong links with the United States. U.S. aid is very important for Israel's **economy**, although much is spent on the military. Israel's other main trading partner is the European Union.

Jobs

There are about 4,000 technology companies in Israel. Manufacturing is also important, as the country produces machinery such as metal-cutting tools. Tourism has at times been affected by the violence in the country. In 2010 over three million tourists visited the country. Israel provides most of its own food, but agriculture is still a fairly small part of the economy. Palestinians are generally less wealthy than Israelis, because they are often unable to get jobs in Israel. It is thought that poverty runs at about 50 percent among Palestinians.

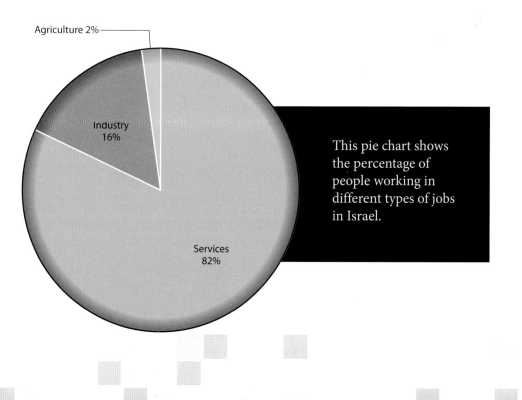

Agriculture 2%

Industry
16%

Services
82%

This pie chart shows the percentage of people working in different types of jobs in Israel.

Wildlife: Nature and Water

The eastern edge of Israel is part of the **migration** route of hundreds of bird **species**. Pelicans and cranes can be seen in places such as Eilat and the Hula Valley. Rare species such as griffon vultures and spotted eagles live in Israel's wildlife reserves.

YOUNG PEOPLE

"Migrating birds know no boundaries" is an educational program set up by the International Center for the Study of Bird Migration in Tel Aviv. More than 300 schools in Israel, 30 in the Palestine Authority, and 30 in Jordan take part in research and education projects. The program helps to bring children from different areas together.

Israel is home to the highly endangered griffon vulture.

Hai Bar

Hai Bar, which means "wildlife," is an organization that aims to protect the country's **endangered** animals and to reintroduce others. Some animals have been bred in captivity (enclosed places such as zoos) and released into the wild. As a result, animals such as the fennec fox and the desert hedgehog are now lower down on endangered animal lists.

Scorpions can be seen in the desert, and Israel is one of the few places where green turtles nest. Snakes and lizards are also common.

Plants

Israel has nearly 3,000 plant species, including desert flowers such as irises in Gilboa reserve and orchids near Jerusalem. Israel is also the only place where a tree called the Euphrates poplar still grows.

How to say...

	Hebrew	**Arabic**
fox	*shoual* (shoo-al)	*ta'lab* (ta'lab)
eagle	*nesher* (ne-sher)	*nasr* (nasr)
snake	*nakhash* (nah-khash)	*af'aa* (af'aa)

The fennec fox is a **conservation** success story.

Timna National Park contains some amazing rocks, including Solomon's pillars.

National parks

Israel has 65 national parks that cover 386 square miles (1,000 square kilometers). The parks are not always vast open spaces. They can also be castles, churches, and caves. There are also 150 nature reserves.

Water conservation

The dry climate means that water conservation is an important issue in Israel. A system of canals, tunnels, and pipelines takes water from Lake Tiberias to the rest of the country. Other projects include **desalination** of seawater. **Irrigation** is a way of watering land or crops in areas that do not get much rainfall. High-tech irrigation has been used to turn desert areas into farmland. Israel pioneered a system of drip irrigation, where narrow pipes with holes are used to drip water onto crops. The system is controlled by computer. Water wastage is only 10 percent. But drip irrigation is expensive, so it is only used on high-value crops, such as fruit, vegetables, and flowers.

Environmental issues

One of the results of Israel's water management systems is that less water reaches the Dead Sea. In addition to this, some companies are **evaporating** Dead Sea water to use the salts in makeup and spa goods. This means that the Dead Sea is disappearing by about 3 feet (1 meter) in depth every year.

Air pollution in Israel often reaches dangerous levels. Also, the huge increase in population in recent years has meant that much land has been taken over by housing and industry.

Agriculture has been made possible in Israel as a result of irrigation systems.

Infrastructure: Parliamentary Democracy

Israel is a **parliamentary democracy**. Citizens elect representatives, who then appoint high-level politicians. Everyone over 18 can vote. The **head of state** is an elected president, but he or she has no real power. The leader of the government is the **prime minister**. He or she is chosen by the president and party leaders. Israel's **parliament**, the Knesset, has 120 members.

The Palestinian Authority

In the West Bank and Gaza, the Palestinians have their own **political parties** and leaders. The **nationalist** Fatah party won the 2005 election for president of the Palestinian Authority. In 2006 the **Islamist** Hamas party won the election for the Legislative Council. Since 2007 Hamas has effectively ruled Gaza, while Fatah has ruled the West Bank.

The Knesset is in Jerusalem.

Jerusalem

Until 1967 the city of Jerusalem was divided into West Jerusalem, controlled by Israel, and East Jerusalem, controlled by Jordan. Israel captured East Jerusalem in the 1967 war. Today, the Palestinians want East Jerusalem to be their capital. Israel currently claims that Jerusalem is their capital city. However, this has not been internationally recognized.

This map shows the six districts of Israel. They are divided into 15 sub-districts.

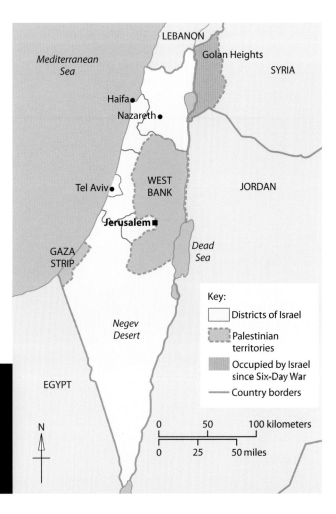

Key:
- Districts of Israel
- Palestinian territories
- Occupied by Israel since Six-Day War
- Country borders

LEBANON
Golan Heights
SYRIA
Mediterranean Sea
Haifa
Nazareth
WEST BANK
Tel Aviv
JORDAN
Jerusalem
Dead Sea
GAZA STRIP
Negev Desert
EGYPT

N

| 0 | 50 | 100 kilometers |
| 0 | 25 | 50 miles |

Daily life

The Hebrew language had not been spoken for many years when Eliezer Ben-Yehuda suggested bringing it back as a spoken language in 1879. Before this it was used only in prayer and studies. Modern Hebrew was accepted as one of three official languages (along with English and Arabic) in British-ruled Palestine in 1921. It was then established as the official language of Israel in 1948. Modern Hebrew is written from right to left, using the 22 letters of the Hebrew alphabet.

The Israeli Defense Force

Israelis must do two or three years of **national service** and do basic reserve duty each year in the Israeli Defense Force (IDF). Their names are then kept on a list, and they are called up to fight if and when necessary. However, many younger people do not like to be forced into national service. They think Israel should have a professional army, like other countries.

Daily life

Some people living in Israeli **settlements** in areas such as the West Bank live very dangerous lives. Palestinians do not like the Israeli settlements, because they believe it shows Israelis will never move out. Settlers often keep a gun at home and travel to work in armored buses. There are attacks made by Palestinians on settlers, and sometimes by settlers on Palestinians.

Health

Israel has several internationally famous hospitals. Medical facilities in the country are often excellent, and both free and private clinics are available. Health tourism is also becoming very popular. Spas based at hot springs or near the Dead Sea are visited by many tourists.

The health properties of the Dead Sea are well known. The mud is good for skin problems.

Media and technology

Many different newspapers, television channels, and radio stations reflect the different cultures in Israel. The Israel Broadcasting Authority provides television and radio channels, and there are commercial and satellite channels available, too.

In 2008, 71.1 percent of Israelis had computers at home, and 90.8 percent of those had an Internet connection. Most cafés and hotels have Internet connections, too. Each household has an average of two cell phones.

Up-to-date technology is common in Israel.

School life

Israeli children go to school from the age of 6 up to the age of 18. Schooling is free. Schools are divided into four types: state schools (where most children go); state religious schools (which focus on Judaism); Arab schools (which focus on Arab history and religion); and private schools (which charge fees). Each year a special topic of national importance, such as the environment, is closely studied.

Secondary education

Secondary education includes **vocational** schools such as technical, military, or agricultural schools. These prepare students for specific jobs. Other secondary schools teach standard subjects such as history and geography.

Higher education

There are world-famous universities in Israel that attract students from around the world. Many Israelis do not begin their studies until at least the age of 21 because of national service, which is three years for men and two for women.

Daily life

Palestinian children have often suffered during the Israel–Palestine conflict. Some have been killed, while others have been harshly treated by Israeli soldiers. Fighting affects schools and health centers. Money and materials have not been available to repair 82 percent of the buildings, so schools have become overcrowded, unhygienic, and unsafe. Education standards for Palestinian children have been falling as a result.

YOUNG PEOPLE

The Re'ut Sadaka movement encourages Israeli Jews and Arabs between the ages of 14 and 18 to meet and become friends. *Re'ut* means "friendship" in Hebrew and Arabic. Jews and Arabs tend to live in different areas and go to different schools. This movement aims to help young people develop an understanding of each other's cultures.

These Muslim and Jewish school children are at the Bible Lands Museum in Jerusalem. They are taking part in a program that aims to bring together Jews and Muslims by focusing on their shared history.

Culture: Food, Music, and Sports

Israelis love *Mizrahi* (Eastern music sung in Hebrew), rock, and pop music. Palestinian rap is popular and focuses on issues such as the occupation of their land by the Israelis. There is a strong classical music tradition, partly as a result of European Jews bringing their love of classical music with them. The Israeli Philharmonic Orchestra is known worldwide.

Famous theaters can be found in Tel Aviv and Jerusalem. The Habima Theater in Tel Aviv is probably the most important and is considered the national theater of Israel. Plays that comment on political issues are often as popular as the musicals brought in from the United States or United Kingdom.

The national dance in Israel is a circle dance called the *hora*. It is often performed at weddings and other celebrations.

Literature

The International Jerusalem Book Fair is attended by people from more than 40 countries. People come to see who wins the celebrated Jerusalem Prize for Literature. Amos Oz, A. B. Yehoshua, and David Grossman are well-known Israeli writers. Palestinians such as Sahar Khalifeh have written about the hardships of Palestinian women's lives.

The Azrieli Center is one of the most modern buildings in Tel Aviv. It houses the biggest shopping center in the city.

Movie industry

Several Israeli movies have been in the running for Academy Awards, such as *Waltz with Bashir* (2008). Haifa and Jerusalem hold international film festivals every year. The Steven Spielberg Film Archive in the Hebrew University of Jerusalem has the world's largest collection of Jewish and Israeli films.

Sports

Soccer and basketball are the most popular sports in Israel, but mountain biking and other outdoor sports are also enjoyed. The Maccabiah Games, held in Israel every four years for Jewish athletes from around the world, are a major cultural event.

A dark day in Israeli sports history took place in 1972. At the Olympics in Munich, Germany, two Israeli athletes were killed and nine others kidnapped by Palestinian **terrorists**. Israel's participation in the Olympics had been seen as a huge step toward repairing relations with Germany after the Holocaust, but things went horribly wrong. The terrorists demanded Palestinian prisoners be freed, but Israel refused. By the end of the day, all 11 Israelis were killed in a shoot-out.

At the Beijing Olympic Games in 2008, Israel played China in the men's wheelchair basketball competition.

Women

Many women in Israel lead lives similar to Americans, working and raising small families. The Women's Equal Rights law was passed in 1951. This gives women equality with men by law, but sometimes religious views may counteract this. Women from **Orthodox** Jewish families often have a stricter, more traditional lifestyle. Many stay at home, as they tend to have large families, although some may teach or work in an office.

YOUNG PEOPLE

Israeli families love camping—for example, by the Sea of Galilee beaches. Those on the eastern coast are particularly popular with teenagers. They camp, swim, and have barbecues. Gan Hashlosha National Park (Sahne) is a popular spot for children to go swimming and have picnics. It has a natural pool fed by **aquifers** that is warm all year round.

Sahne National Park is a beautiful place to visit.

Religion

More than three-quarters of Israel's population is Jewish. Most are not regular worshippers, but there are many Orthodox Jews who observe the Jewish religion in every detail. Shabbat (Saturday) is a day of rest for Jewish people, and in many places everything shuts down. Some people avoid doing any work, traveling by car, or even answering the telephone on Shabbat.

Food and meals

Popular Israeli foods include olives, grapes, apricots, and other fruits, as well as hummus and falafel. One of the favorite meals is chicken soup with matzah meal dumplings, called matzah balls.

Israelis usually eat their main meal at noon, when children are home from school. The evening meal consists of salads and dairy foods. Israelis often eat a large breakfast, which includes salad, cheese, olives, bread, and coffee.

There are some rules about food, called **Kosher** laws, that Jewish people are supposed to follow. For example, they are not allowed to eat pork, and meat and dairy foods cannot be stored or cooked together. The Palestinian territories are mainly Muslim, and they also do not eat pork. Muslims are not supposed to drink alcohol.

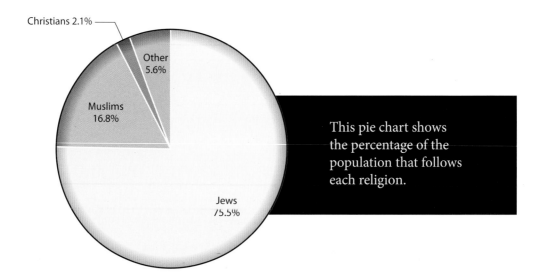

Christians 2.1%

Other 5.6%

Muslims 16.8%

Jews 75.5%

This pie chart shows the percentage of the population that follows each religion.

Falafel

Ask an adult to help you make this tasty snack.

Ingredients

- 14.5-ounce can chickpeas
- 1 large onion, chopped
- 2 garlic cloves, chopped
- 3 tablespoons fresh parsley, chopped
- 1 teaspoon ground coriander
- 1 teaspoon cumin
- Salt and pepper
- 2 tablespoons flour
- Sunflower or vegetable oil

What to do

1. Drain the chickpeas, place them in a saucepan with fresh water, and bring them to a boil. Boil for 5 minutes, then simmer on low for about 10 minutes, so the chickpeas become a little softer.
2. Drain the chickpeas and allow them to cool for 15 minutes.
3. Combine the chickpeas, onion, garlic, parsley, coriander, cumin, salt, and pepper in a medium-sized bowl.
4. Mash the ingredients together with a fork until they are a rough paste. Add the flour.
5. Mold the mixture into small balls, each one about the size of a Ping-Pong ball. Slightly flatten each ball.
6. Fry in about 3 inches (8 centimeters) of oil at a temperature of 350 °F (180 °C) until golden brown (for about 4 minutes). Remove with a slotted spoon and drain on paper towels. Serve hot or cold.

Israel Today

Israel has come a long way since 1948. Its population has grown enormously. The **immigration** of skilled workers has helped the **economy** to develop. Tourism is increasing, despite fears about safety. The religious importance of Jerusalem means that religious people will always travel to Israel. Many Israelis are proud of the way they have built their country up from poor beginnings to a nation with living standards roughly equal to those in Western Europe.

It is true, however, that like many Western countries, there is a widening gap between rich and poor. Many Palestinian **refugees** still live in refugee camps in Arab countries (except in Jordan). There were at least four million of these refugees in 2010. This is just one of the many issues that Israelis and Arabs will need to address if the peace process is to end positively.

Hope for peace

At the end of 2010, peace talks were continuing. The hope is that eventually an Israeli state and a Palestinian state can exist side by side. Violence and **suicide bombers** may become a thing of the past. How long it will take to get there is impossible to know, but most people hope that peace comes soon.

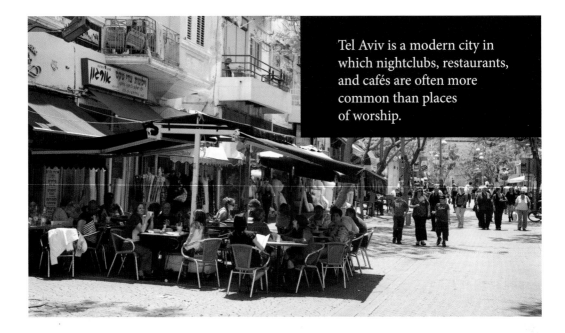

Tel Aviv is a modern city in which nightclubs, restaurants, and cafés are often more common than places of worship.

The Western Wall is a place of **pilgrimage** for Jews. They write prayers on pieces of paper and stick them in gaps in the wall.

Fact File

Name:	State of Israel
Government:	**parliamentary democracy**
Area:	8,522 square miles (22,072 square kilometers), including Jerusalem and Golan
Bordering countries:	Lebanon; Syria; Jordan; Egypt
Capital:	Jerusalem (not internationally recognized)
Largest city:	Jerusalem
Population:	7,473,052 (July 2010 est.)
Life expectancy at birth:	79 (men); 83 (women)
Languages:	Hebrew; Arabic
Currency:	1 New Israeli Shekel (ILS) = 100 new agorot
Religion:	Judaism and Islam, with minority Christian
Longest river:	Jordan River, at 224 miles (360 kilometers)
Highest point:	Mount Meron, at 3,963 feet (1,208 meters)
Lowest point:	Dead Sea, at 1,312 feet (400 meters) below sea level
Coastline:	170 miles (273 kilometers)
Imports:	military equipment; grain; fuels; rough diamonds
Exports:	computer software; cut diamonds; minerals; paper products; chemicals; military equipment; citrus fruits

Public holidays

Jewish people use the Jewish or Hebrew calendar for religious purposes. It is based on 12 lunar months (354 days), but with an extra month added every few years so that it matches the solar year (365 days). A Jewish holiday falls on the same day of every Jewish calendar year. This is why it appears in different months in the calendar (called the Gregorian calendar) used by most of the Western world.

These Jewish public holidays fall in the following months:
February/March: Purim
March/April: Passover
April/May: Holocaust Memorial Day; National Memorial Day; Independence Day
May/June: Shavuot
July/August: Tisha B'Av
September: Rosh Hashanah
September/October: Yom Kippur; Sukkot; Simhat Torah
December: Hannukah

The Dead Sea is so salty that piles of salt form in the water and on the coast.

National anthem: "*Hatikva*" ("The Hope")

As long as deep in the heart,
The soul of a Jew yearns,
And forward to the East
To Zion, an eye looks
Our hope will not be lost,
The hope of two thousand years,
To be a free nation in our land,
The land of Zion and Jerusalem.

How to say...

Hebrew

Monday	*yom sheni*	(yom-shey-nee)
Tuesday	*yom shlishi*	(yom-shlee-shee)
Wednesday	*yom revi'i*	(yom-re-vee-ee)
Thursday	*yom khamishi*	(yom-kha-mee-shee)
Friday	*yom shishi*	(yom-shee-shee)
Saturday	*shabbat*	(sha-bat)
Sunday	*yom rishon*	(yom ree-shon)

Arabic

Monday	*yom al-itneen*	(yawm al-itnayn)
Tuesday	*yom al-talaata*	(yawm al-talaata)
Wednesday	*yom al-arba'a*	(yawm al-arba'a)
Thursday	*yom al-khamees*	(yawm al-khamees)
Friday	*yom al-jum'a*	(yawm al-jum'a)
Saturday	*yom al-sabt*	(yawm al-sabt)
Sunday	*yom al-ahad*	(yawm al-ahad)

GOLDA MEIR (1898-1978)

Golda Meir was born in Kiev, Ukraine. She trained as a teacher in the United States, but in her twenties she traveled to what would become Israel, to live on a **kibbutz**. She was active in politics for many years. At the age of 70, she became **prime minister** and led Israel during the Yom Kippur War of 1973. The war did not go well, and she resigned a few months after the end of the war. She died of cancer in 1978.

Timeline

BCE means "before the common era." When this appears after a date, it refers to the number of years before the Christian religion began. BCE dates are always counted backward.

CE means "common era." When this appears after a date, it refers to the time after the Christian religion began.

before 1250 BCE	Jews first live in the area now known as Israel.
66–70 CE	The first Jewish War against the Romans begins.
70	Jewish people are forced out of Jerusalem by Titus and the Roman army, who destroy the Second Temple.
135	The Bar-Kokhba revolt occurs.
638	Arabs conquer Jerusalem.
1099	Jews are massacred by the Crusaders conquering Jerusalem.
1897	Theodor Herzel forms the **Zionist** movement.
1917	The Balfour Declaration says there will be a national home created for Jews in Palestine.
1921	The **League of Nations** gives **mandates** to Britain and France to rule the area now known as Israel.
1939–45	World War II sees the killing of six million Jews, in what is known as the Holocaust.
1947	The British hand control of Palestine to the **United Nations**.
1948	David Ben-Gurion proclaims the independent State of Israel. Hebrew becomes the official language of Israel.
May 1948– Jan 1949	The first Arab-Israeli War occurs.
1967	The Six-Day War begins, in which Israel occupies the West Bank, Gaza Strip, East Jerusalem, Golan Heights, and Sinai Peninsula.
1972	Eleven Israeli staff and athletes are kidnapped and killed at the Munich Olympics.
1973	The Yom Kippur War between Israel and Egypt occurs.

1978	Israel and Egypt agree to peace.
1980	Israel announces that Jerusalem is the capital of Israel.
1982	Israel invades Lebanon.
1987	The first **Intifada** begins.
1990s	There is a huge increase in Jewish **immigration** to Israel from states of the former Soviet Union.
1993	Israel and Palestinians sign the Oslo Accords.
1995	**Prime Minister** Yitzhak Rabin is killed by a Jewish **extremist**.
2000	Israeli troops withdraw from Lebanon. The Second Intifada begins.
2002	Israel builds a wall around parts of the West Bank.
2005	Ariel Sharon, the Likud prime minister, sets up a new party called Kadima; Israelis leave Gaza and four **settlements** in the northern West Bank. Citizens who do not leave voluntarily are forced out.
2006	Hamas wins the Palestinian Authority election.
2006	Israel attacks Lebanon over the kidnapping of an Israeli soldier.
2007	Hamas take over Gaza.
2008	Peace talks break down as Israel launches an attack on Gaza, in response to what the Israelis say was Palestinian rocket fire.
2010	Peace talks restart in Washington, D.C., under the guidance of the United States.
2011	Hamas and Fatah begin talks.

Glossary

aquifer underground lake of water

cease-fire agreement to stop fighting during a war

concentration camp place in which large numbers of people, often minorities such as Jews in World War II, are imprisoned. The camps are usually crowded with very basic facilities.

conservation looking after things such as animals or the environment to prevent them from being damaged or destroyed

desalination way of making sea water drinkable by removing the salt from it

economy relating to money and the industry and jobs in a country

endangered when animals or plants are seriously at risk of dying out

evaporate heat a liquid until it becomes a gas

extremist person who holds extreme political or religious views

gas chamber airtight room that can be filled with poisonous gas. Gas chambers were used by the Nazis in World War II to kill Jewish people.

head of state person who represents a country. Sometimes this person is also the leader of the country.

immigration act of coming to live in a foreign country

Intifada Palestinian uprising against the Israeli occupation of the West Bank and Gaza Strip

irrigation way of watering land or crops in areas that do not get much rainfall

Islamist favoring an extreme form of Islam

kibbutz settlement—often a farm—in which people work and live together, sharing everything

Kosher set of rules for the way food must be prepared and eaten by Jewish people

League of Nations organization of countries set up to promote peace

mandate official order to do something

migration move from one habitat to another, depending on the season

national service period of time that each person has to spend in the army

nationalist person who wants independence for his or her country

Orthodox conforming strictly to a set of traditions or religious beliefs

parliament ruling body of some countries; laws are made there

parliamentary democracy system of government in which citizens elect representatives, and these representatives, in turn, appoint high-level politicians such as the prime minister

pilgrimage journey to a place of particular interest, usually a religious place

political party group of people who believe in the same things. A political party is an organization that tries to gain power in the government.

prime minister head of a parliamentary government

refugee person who has been forced to leave his or her country because of war or persecution

resources means available for a country to develop, such as minerals and energy sources

rift valley steep-sided valley

right-wing holding conservative values and not wanting change

settlement place where people set up a community

species type of animal, bird, or fish

stateless when a person is not recognized as a member of any country, which means he or she does not have the rights of a citizen

suicide bomber person who plans a bomb attack on other people or a place and who expects to die from the attack himself or herself

terrorist person who uses violence to achieve a political aim

trade buying and selling goods and services

United Nations (UN) organization of countries set up to promote peace. The United Nations took over from the League of Nations in 1945.

vocational relating to a particular job

Zionist relating to a movement with the aim to re-establish a Jewish nation

Find Out More

Books

Bowden, Rob. *The Middle East and North Africa* (*Regions of the World*). Chicago: Heinemann Library, 2008.

Gallagher, Michael. *Israel* (*Countries in the News*). North Mankato, Minn.: Smart Apple Media, 2008.

Hodge, Susie. *Israel* (*Changing World*). North Mankato, Minn.: Smart Apple Media, 2009.

King, John. *Israel and Palestine* (*The Middle East*). Chicago: Raintree, 2006.

Steele, Philip. *The Atlas of People and Places*. Brookfield, Conn.: Copper Beech, 2002.

Young, Emma. *Israel* (*Countries of the World*). Washington, D.C.: National Geographic, 2008.

Websites

www.israelemb.org/kids/home_page.html
Find out lots of information about Israel on this site.

www.uri.org/kids/world_juda.htm
This website will help you to learn more about Judaism.

Places to visit

If you go to Israel, these are some of the places you could visit:

The Dead Sea
You can read a book while floating here, or have a mud bath!

Masada National Park
Either take a cable car or walk along the Snake Path to the top of Masada, the ancient fortress that overlooks the Dead Sea.

The Dome of the Rock

The beautiful decoration of the Dome is well worth seeing.

Tower of David Museum

www.towerofdavid.org.il/English/General/Tower_of_David-Museum_of_the_History_of_Jerusalem

Visit this museum to learn about the history of Jerusalem.

Sea of Galilee

You can go on a boat ride to see the historic sites around the lake, or visit the Crusader Castle perched high above the Sea of Galilee.

Haifa

Haifa is built on a hill. You can go for a tram ride down the hillside, have a picnic in National Park Carmel, or go horseback riding for the day.

Eilat

Eilat has beautiful beaches and lots of water sports. You can also visit Dolphin Reef to see the dolphins or go on a hike by camel.

Coral Beach Nature Reserve

This is Israel's only coral reef. You can see underwater gardens of coral and some beautifully colored fish.

Topic Tools

You can use these topic tools for your school projects. Trace the map onto a sheet of paper, using the thick black outline to guide you.

Israel's flag was adopted in 1948. The Star of David has long been an important symbol for Jews. The blue and white colors come from the Jewish prayer shawl. Copy the flag design and then color in your picture. Make sure you use the right colors!

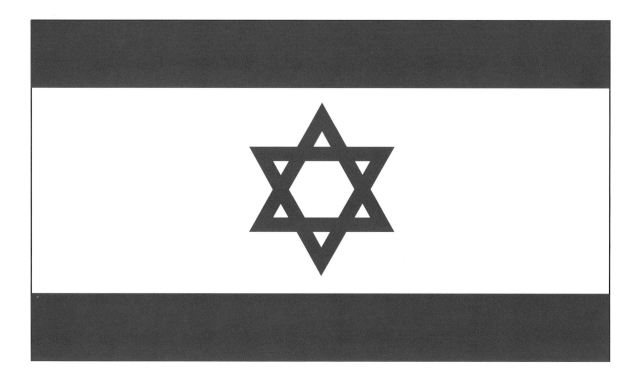

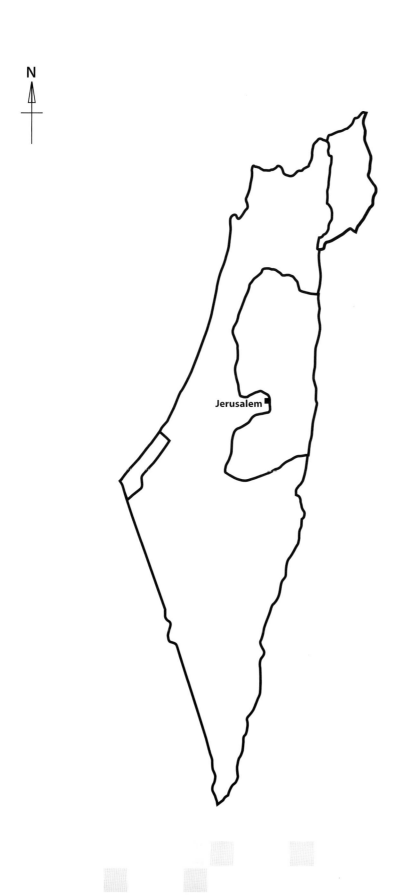

N

Jerusalem

Index

Titles in the series